I0415798

U.S. Department
of Transportation

**National Highway
Traffic Safety
Administration**

Child Restraint Dynamic Performance Evaluation in a 48 km/h (30 mph) Sled Test

Technical Report
May 2005

U.S. Department
of Transportation

**National Highway
Traffic Safety
Administration**

Memorandum

Subject: Child Restraint Dynamic Performance Evaluation
in a 48 km/h (30 mph) Sled Test

Date:

From: Sean Doyle
Engineer, New Car Assessment Division

Reply to
Attn. of:

To: NHTSA Docket 2004-18682

THRU: Nathaniel Beuse
Division Chief, New Car Assessment Division

Roger A. Saul
Director, Office of Crashworthiness Standards

Jacqueline Glassman
Chief Counsel

Please submit the attached technical report titled "Child Restraint Dynamic Performance
Evaluation in a 48 km/h (30 mph) Sled Test" to NHTSA Docket 2004-18682. This report
is a summary of child dummy data obtained from FY 2003 sled testing conducted under
the New Car Assessment Program.

Attachment
"Child Restraint Dynamic Performance Evaluation
in a 48 km/h (30 mph) Sled Test"

SAFETY BELTS SAVE LIVES

Get it together!

Table of Contents

Technical Report Documentation Page

1. Report No. 2004-01	2. Government Accession No.	3. Recipients Catalog No.		
4. Title and Subtitle Child Restraint Dynamic Performance Evaluation In a 48 km/h (30 MPH) Sled Test		5. Report Date TBD, 2004		
		6. Performing Organization Code NVS-111		
7. Author(s) Lauren Beauchamp, Nathaniel Beuse, Sean Doyle		8. Performing Organization Report No.		
9. Performing Organization Name and Address U.S. Department of Transportation National Highway Traffic Safety Administration Rulemaking Office of Crashworthiness Standards		10. Work Unit No.		
		11. Contract or Grant No.		
12. Sponsoring Agency Name and Address U.S. Department of Transportation National Highway Traffic Safety Administration Rulemaking Office of Crashworthiness Standards Mail Code: NVS-111 400 Seventh Street, SW, Room 5307 Washington, D.C. 20590		13. Type of Report and Period Covered Final Report		
		14. Sponsoring Agency Code NHTSA		
15. Supplementary Notes				

16. Abstract

In response to the TREAD Act, the agency implemented a pilot program designed to investigate the feasibility of rating child restraints based on dynamic performance. This was accomplished by subjecting child restraints to a 48 km/h (30 mph) sled test under the same test conditions as the FMVSS No. 213 standard (49 CFR Part 571), final rule published June 24th, 2003. The child restraints were tested in various configurations and occupied by dummies of various sizes. The pilot program was conducted under the New Car Assessment Program (NCAP). Results showed little variance between different child restraints tested in the same configuration; however, a more substantial, statistically significant, difference in HIC performance was observed between different configurations of the same child restraint. These results indicate that the agency cannot assume similar results for different configurations of the same child restraint. Most of the dummy injury values fell well under the current injury assessment reference values published in FMVSS No. 213.

| 17. Key Words

New Car Assessment Program (NCAP)
FMVSS No. 213
Child Restraint System (CRS)
Indicant Compliance Testing | | 18. Distribution Statement

Copies of this report are available from:

National Highway Traffic Safety Admin.
NHTSA Technical Reference Division
400 Seventh St., SW, Room 5108
Washington, DC 20590 | | |
| 19. Security Classification (of this report)

UNCLASSIFIED | | 20. Security Classification (of this page)

UNCLASSIFIED | 21. No. of Pages | 22. Price |

I. <u>BACKGROUND</u>:

In November 2000, Congress directed the Secretary of Transportation to develop a child restraint safety rating system that is practicable and understandable (Section 14 (g) of the Transportation Recall Enhancement, Accountability, and Documentation (TREAD) Act, November 1, 2000, Pub.L. 106-414, 114 Stat. 1800) and that will help consumers to make informed decisions when purchasing child restraints. The responsibility of this mandate fell to the National Highway Traffic Safety Administration (NHTSA), which published a final rule on November 6, 2002 announcing its intent to establish a consumer information program for add-on child restraints based on ease of use. In addition, the agency announced it would conduct two, two-year pilot programs to gather additional information on child passenger safety. One pilot program was designed to investigate the feasibility of rating vehicles on how well they protect children, by installing child safety seats in the rear seats of vehicles tested in the existing frontal New Car Assessment Program (NCAP) vehicle tests. The second pilot program was designed to investigate the feasibility of a rating based on a child restraint's dynamic performance. This was accomplished by subjecting child restraints to a 48 km/h (30 mph) sled test under the same test conditions as the new Federal Motor Vehicle Safety Standard (FMVSS) No. 213 (49 CFR 571.213), final rule published June 24, 2003. This report will summarize and analyze the data from the Fiscal Year (FY) 2003 NCAP child restraint dynamic performance testing program. The results of this pilot program are made available only as research, and no ratings are assigned to any of the child restraint systems (CRS) tested.

II. METHODOLGY:

As specified in Standard No. 213, 49 CFR §571.213, the agency does compliance testing of child restraints on a sled buck at a nominal speed of 48 km/h (30 mph). Currently, the TNO dummy is used in testing to represent a 9-month-old infant, and the Hybrid II family of dummies is used in testing to represent a 3-year-old (3YO) child and 6-year-old (6YO) child. Only the 3-year-old and 6-year-old dummies are instrumented. NHTSA published a notice of proposed rulemaking May 1, 2002 (67 FR 21806, Docket No. NHTSA-2002-11707), proposing a number of revisions to FMVSS No. 213, including the incorporation of more advanced test dummies, updated injury criteria, and minor revisions to the test bench and sled pulse. On November 5, 2002 (67 FR 214 Docket No. NHTSA-2001-10053), NHTSA proposed using the updated test bench assembly and more advanced test dummies proposed by the FMVSS No. 213 NPRM for the CRS dynamic rating pilot study.

The main goal of this pilot program was to test for statistically significant results when comparing different child restraints in different configurations. As such, the testing included various sized child dummies, child seat anchoring methods (i.e. Lower Anchors and Tethers for Children (LATCH) vs. lap belt) and child seat setups (i.e. forward-facing vs. rear-facing). The current compliance test procedure for FMVSS No. 213 specifies a single child restraint in the center seating position (P6) per sled test. However, for the CRS dynamic rating pilot study, the agency sought to test two child restraints on the sled bench at once, allowing for a direct-paired comparison test between two different CRS configurations and shortening the time for testing.[1] In order to test two child restraints on the sled bench per run it was necessary to move the child restraints out of the customary P6 seating position to the outboard seating positions (P3 and P4). However, because there are no lower LATCH anchors for the outboard seating positions P3 and P4 on the sled bench, to eliminate any variability, the P3 and P4 seating positions on the bench were fitted with lower anchorage points that had the same locations as the P6 seating position[2]. Figure 1 illustrates the seating positions P1 – P6 in a passenger vehicle. The test bench for the sled represents the rear bench seat of a vehicle.

Figure 1

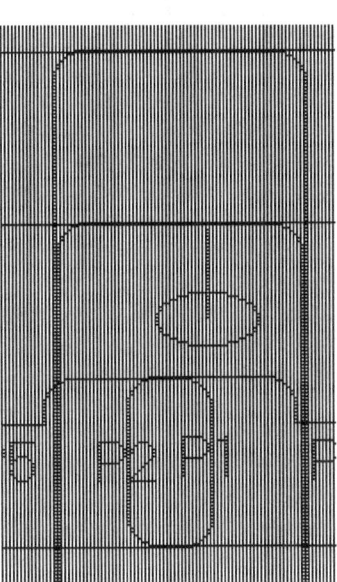

Figure 2 illustrates two child restraints on the sled test bench secured in the P3 and P4 positions.

Figure 2

The analysis presented in this report is largely based on two injury criteria: Head Injury Criteria (HIC) and chest acceleration; however, the agency also analyzed head and knee excursions and neck and pelvis data for all child restraints, as well as child seat rotations for rear-facing child restraints. These are all available in the individual test reports and some are also reported in the content of this technical paper. The HIC and chest acceleration injury criteria were chosen since these measurements have historically been used to assess the probability of injury and because FMVSS No. 213 has Injury Assessment Reference Values (IARV) limits for these two measurements[3].

---

[3] FMVSS No. 213 (49 CFR Part 571) final rule published June 24, 2003

Each child restraint was also subjected to a physical examination after each test was completed. This examination, as outlined in the FMVSS No. 213 testing procedure, evaluated the structural integrity of the child restraint shell, harness, and attachment hardware. A film analysis was also completed post-test to help evaluate kinematical response.

III. <u>EXPERIMENTAL DESIGN</u>:

The two main goals of the pilot study were to 1) statistically compare the dynamic performance between different CRS configurations, and 2) determine the range of dynamic performances across CRS models. The first goal was set to assist the agency in determining whether or not child restraints with multiple configurations (such as an infant seat with and without its base) would have to be tested multiple times to get an accurate representation of the child seat's dynamic performance. Table 1 shows the numerous configurations that typical child restraints can be used in.

Table 1

CRS	Type[4]	Infant	Convert.	Combo 2-in-1	Combo 3-in-1	BPB[5]
Dummy	CRABI[6]	X	X		X	
	3YO		X	X	X	X
	6YO			X	X	X
Orientation	Rear Facing	X	X		X	
	Forward Facing		X	X	X	X
Attachment	LATCH	X	X	X	X	
	Belt w/ Tether		X	X	X	
	Belt Only	X	X	X	X	X
Usage	Base	X				
	No Base	X				

[4] For more detailed information on child restraint types visit please refer to Table A-5 in Appendix A
[5] Belt Positioning Booster
[6] Child Restraint Air Bag Interaction

The second goal was to determine if the agency would see a wide dispersion of dynamic performances across different child restraints. This data would determine whether or not it is feasible to distinguish dynamic performance between different child restraint models to provide meaningful information to consumers.

The test matrix contained 46 sled runs, which resulted in a total of 80 child restraints (40 different models) being tested. These 80 restraints represented a large majority of the seats available in the market at the time of testing. As such, the agency tested various child restraint types, models, and brands in the six different test series. These series included:

1) One child restraint on the sled bench versus two child restraints. This series was done with Hybrid III 3YO dummies in forward-facing child restraints to establish that testing two CRSs in the P3 and P4 seating positions was comparable to testing one dummy in the P6 position.

2) Infant seats with and without their bases (same CRS model per comparison) with CRABI dummies

3) Hybrid III 3YO dummies versus CRABI dummies in rear-facing child restraints (same CRS model per comparison)

4) Hybrid III 3YO dummies versus CRABI dummies in forward-facing child restraints (same CRS model per comparison)

5) Child restraints with a lap belt and top tether versus LATCH

6) Hybrid III 3YO dummies in belt-positioning booster seats versus Hybrid III 6YO dummies in belt-positioning boosters.

In total, the agency tested 6 infant restraint models that could be used with a base or without, 17 convertible child restraint models, 9 combination child restraint models, and 8 belt-positioning booster seats.

A) Statistical Design:

The test matrix was designed to perform paired t-tests, which controlled all differences within a test except the variable of interest. Given the large number of dummy-CRS combinations, it was important to test as many combinations as possible yet have a sample size that was able to make meaningful statistical comparisons. The formula for the confidence interval is plus or minus the estimated standard error of the test results multiplied by a constant that depends on the sample size. The sample is based on a conventional 95% confidence interval. Larger samples are generally better, but the effect diminishes as the sample size grows.

The sled test matrix of dummies and child seat configurations was designed so that comparisons could be made with statistical confidence. Given the large number of dummy-child restraint configuration combinations and the limited number of tests, it was important to test as many combinations as possible yet have enough samples to draw statistically sound conclusions. Typically, it is difficult to determine if differences based on a small number of tests are statistically significant. One method for dealing with small sample size is the use of paired tests. Paired tests enable one to implicitly control for factors other than performance differences. The first test series was designed to determine any disparity in the dynamic performance of a child restraint when it is the only restraint on the sled bench as opposed to being one of two restraints on the sled bench. A paired t-test was used to analyze the observed difference in the dynamic performance of one particular seat on the sled versus the same restraint on the sled with another restraint. Comparing the performance of the same restraint in both tests controls any differences across seats. The remaining five test series were performed using paired t-tests where the results from the P3 and P4 positions on the sled bench were paired. Considering the power of the paired t-test, it was determined that a minimum of six samples would be adequate to establish comparison significance.

IV. TEST RESULTS:

A) One CRS vs. Two CRS on Sled Bench:

Four child restraints were chosen, two convertible seats and two combination seats, with four different child seat manufacturers represented. Each child restraint model was tested twice, once in the P6 position on the sled bench by itself, and a second time in one of the outboard positions (P3 or P4) alongside another child restraint. All child restraints were secured using LATCH and tested with a Hybrid III 3YO dummy. Both HIC and chest acceleration data were analyzed and no statistical difference was observed between the number of child restraints on the sled bench and the injury values accrued. Figures 3 and 4 show the HIC and chest acceleration values respectively for the four restraints tested in the two configurations. These two figures, along with all the other HIC and chest acceleration figures in this report, have been normalized to the FMVSS No. 213 injury limits of 1000 and 60 respectively. Head and knee excursions, found in table 2, were also compared for this test series and again no significant differences were found between those measurements. All restraints would have passed the structural evaluation of FMVSS No. 213 except for one restraint which had a tether release during the test.[7] Post-test analysis assured the agency that the tether release did not occur because two child restraints were on the sled bench. Although the tether release is not considered a failure at this time because the child restraints were tested per future FMVSS No. 213 procedures, the tether release remained a concern, therefore the Office of Enforcement was informed of the occurrence. Enforcement was also informed of all other CRS's that failed this pilot program according to the future FMVSS No. 213 standard.

From the analysis of this test series, the agency made a determination that for the remaining five series of sled tests it would be appropriate to test two child restraints on each sled run.

Table 2

One CRS vs. Two CRS					
		Head Excursion* (mm)		Knee Excursion** (mm)	
Restraint	Type	One	Two	One	Two
Cosco Summit	Combination	561	572	701	678
Evenflo Express	Combination	503	513	635	671
Century 1500 STE	Convertible	572	551	645	660
Britax Marathon	Convertible	551*	417	650***	594

*FMVSS No. 213 Head Excursion limit: 720 mm with top tether, 813 mm without top tether
**FMVSS No. 213 Knee Excursion limit: 914 mm
*** Tether Release

---

[7] Britax Marathon model # E9L0636. Hook released from anchor.

Figure 3

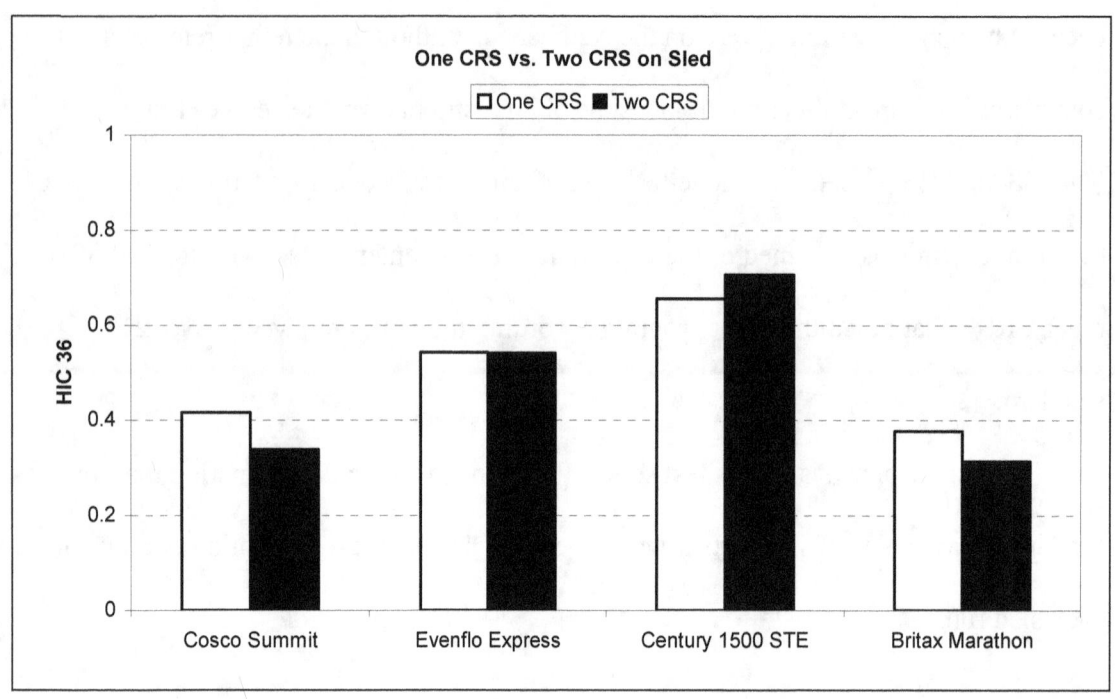

Figure 4

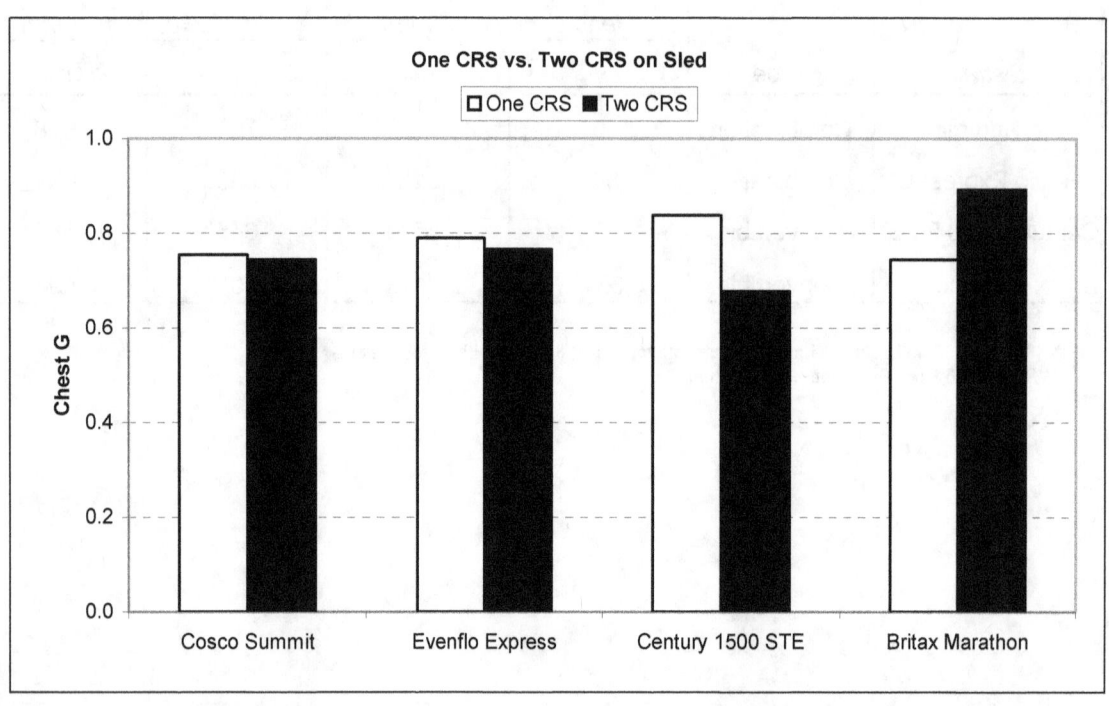

B) **Base vs. No Base:**

Several child restraint manufacturers produce infant seats that have a removable base, and the majority of them can be used in vehicles with or without it. Comparisons were made using HIC and chest acceleration data for the same child restraint model with and without its removable base. Head and knee excursions are not measured for rear-facing configurations; however, CRS seat back rotation is measured using stadia poles.[8] Each child restraint was positioned rear-facing with a CRABI dummy and lower anchorages. Six different infant restraint models were tested representing three different child restraint manufacturers. The agency tested models with both three-point and five-point harnesses in order to ensure an accurate analysis of different infant restraints available on the market. There was no performance comparison made between the three-point and five-point harnesses because the variable of interest in this series was the usage of the infant restraint with or without its removable base. The agency tested both harness types because FMVSS No. 213 compliance test results show HIC and chest acceleration differences between harness types, and neither of the two harness types always performs better than the other.[9] On each sled run, the same infant restraint model was positioned in the P3 and P4 position. The P3 position always contained the infant restraint with the base and the P4 position contained the same restraint without its base. Testing showed a statistical difference in HIC values for the CRABI dummy when testing the restraint with the base versus without the base.[10] This comparison can be seen in Figure 5. The agency did not observe any statistical difference in chest acceleration values between the base and no base configurations, which can be seen in Figure 6.

---

[8] These are graduated poles intercepted by two parallel cross hairs used to survey distances by noting intervals
[9] FMVSS No. 213 test results can be found at www.nhtsa.dot.gov/cars/testing/comply/fmvss213/index.html
[10] Statistical difference at the 95% confidence interval (.05 level)

Figure 5

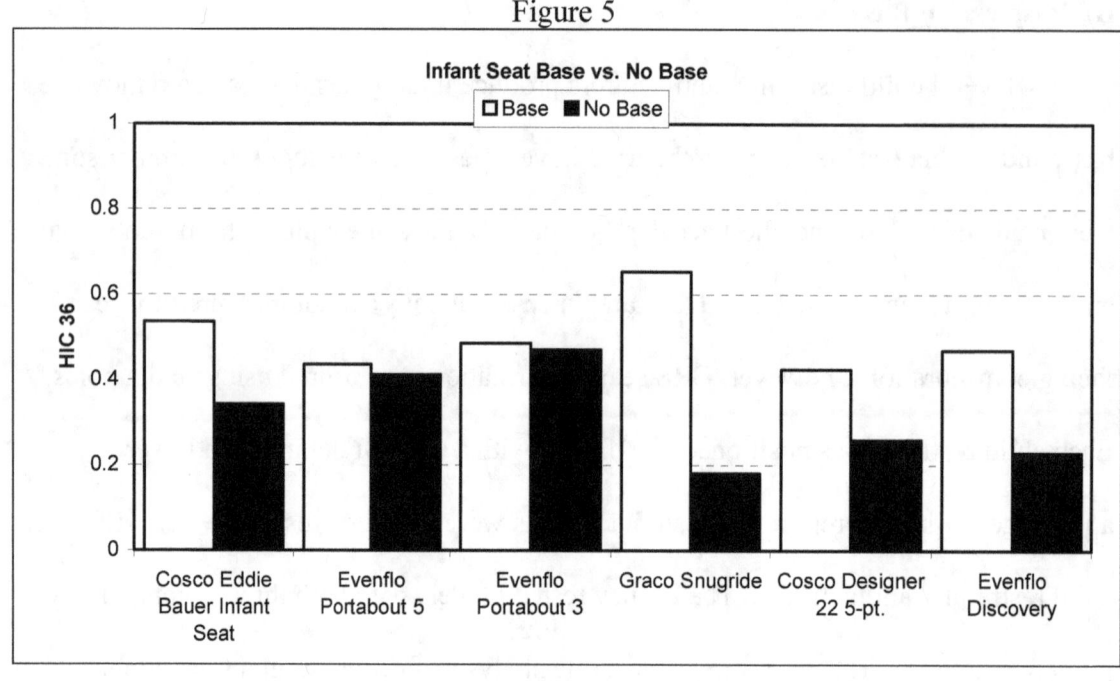

In four of the tests, the agency saw a difference in the HIC response of the

CRABI for the two different configurations. The best example of this difference could be

Figure 6

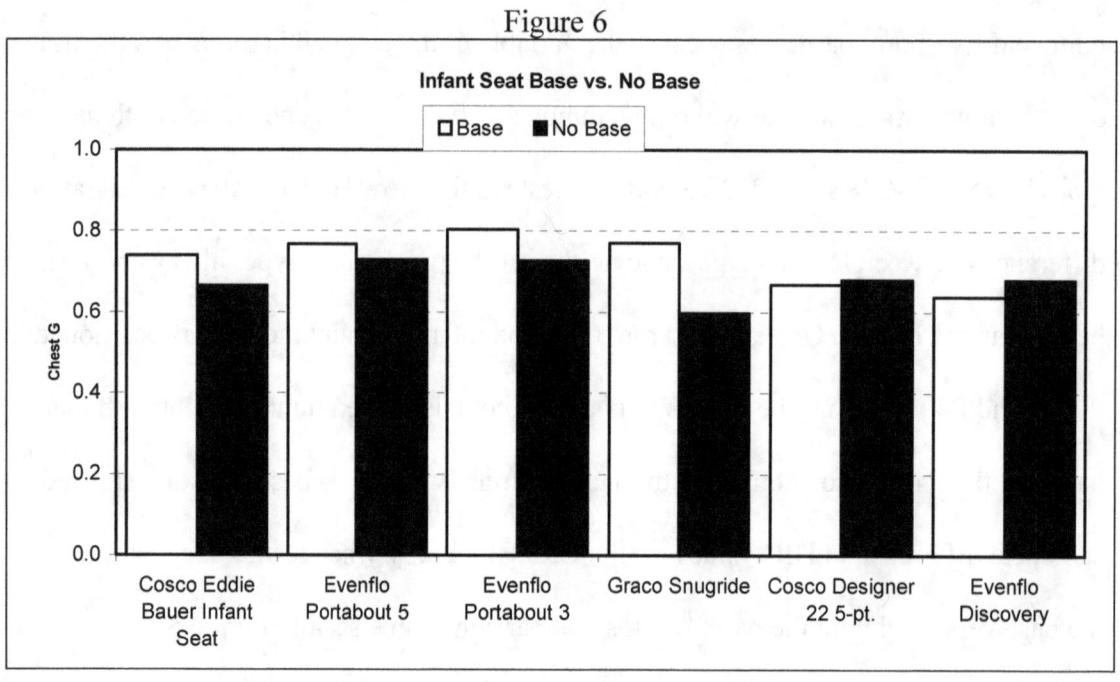

seen in the Graco Snugride test. Plotting the head "x"[11] velocities of the two

configurations along with the sled velocity shows that the CRABI dummy restrained in

the infant seat without the base more closely follows the sled pulse than the CRABI

dummy restrained in the infant seat with the base. In fact, by comparing the initial slope

between the two configurations it becomes apparent that the head "x" velocity for the no

base configuration is almost parallel to the slope of the sled, where the head x velocity of

the restraint with the base has a much steeper initial slope. This same trend can be seen

in most of the base versus no base comparisons for HIC.

Figure 7
Graco Snugride Velocity Plots

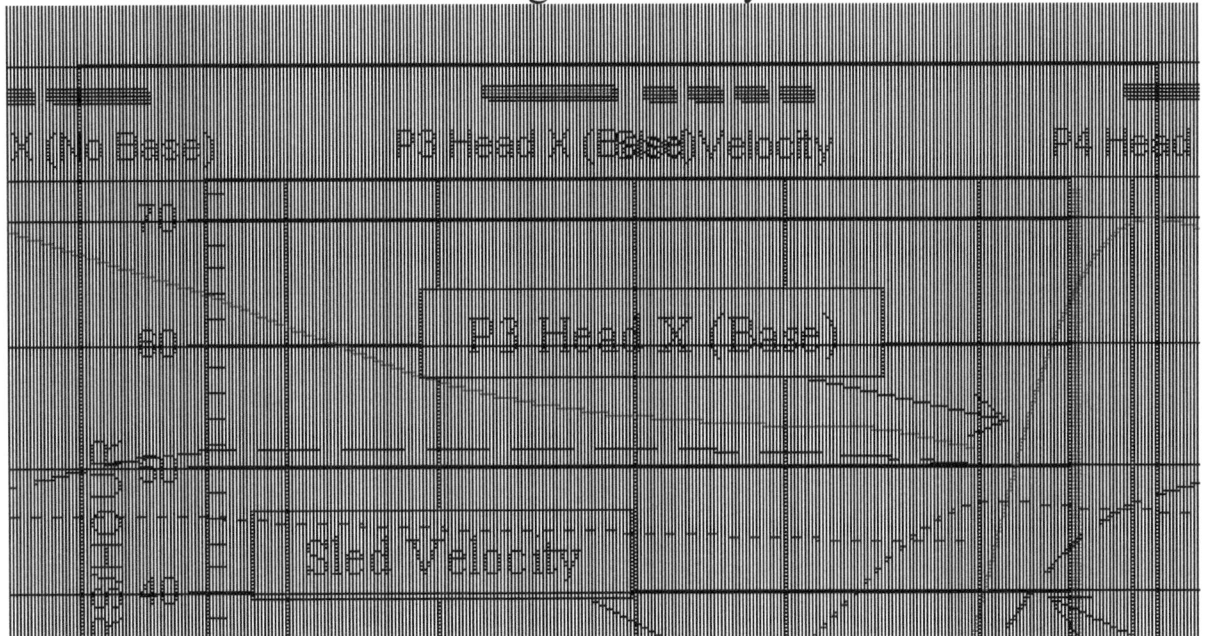

---

[11] The coordinate system for the dummy is as follows: X direction is forward and backward movement; Y direction is lateral movement, and Z direction is vertical movement.

When examining the physical dimensions of the two configurations, it is apparent that the inclusion of the base with the infant restraint affects the geometry of the restraint. The dummy restrained in the infant seat with the base sits higher up in relation to the lower anchorages, which also act as the pivot point, and appear to result in a greater moment across this point during the event. This higher seating position may in part account for the different kinematic responses (greater seat back rotation and slightly delayed dummy responses in the restraints with the base compared to the restraints without the base) seen between the base and no base configurations. This can be seen in Figure 8, which shows a pretest photograph of two infant restraints of the same make and model, one with its removable base attached (Background) and one with it removed (Foreground).

Figure 8

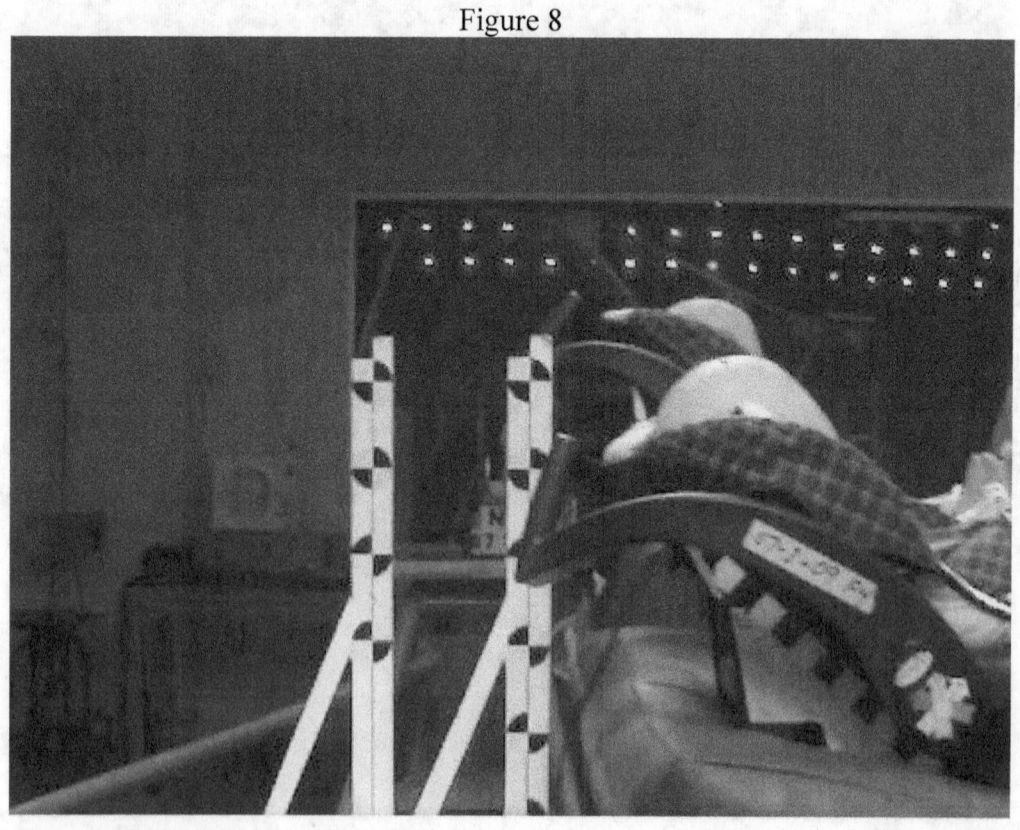

The rotation of the child seat was also investigated and, although none of the seats tested exceeded the maximum seat back rotation angle allowed by FMVSS No. 213, a trend (shown in Table 3) can been seen between higher HIC values and greater seat back rotation. FMVSS No. 213 regulates that a rear-facing child restraint fails compliance if it exceeds a seat back rotation angle of greater than 70° from vertical.[12] Further analysis showed that all except one of the infant seats tested had lower seat rotation when tested without the base.

Figure 9

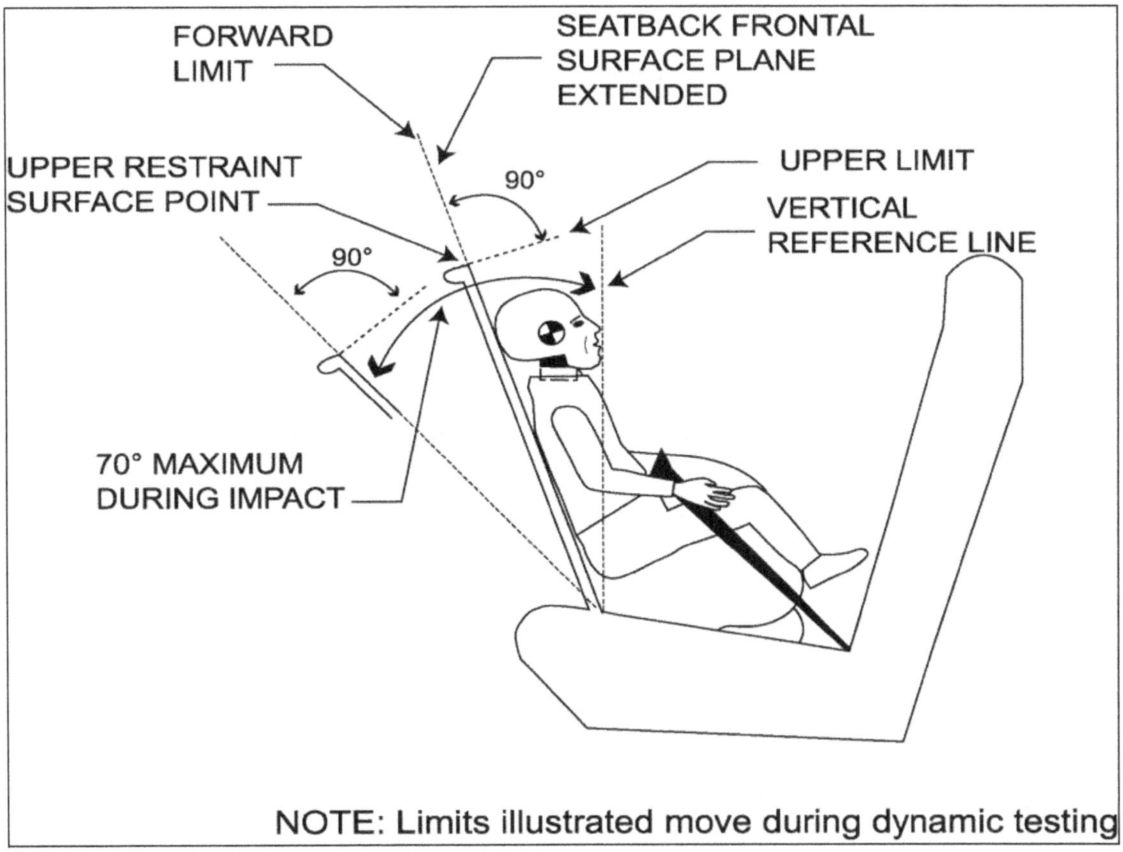

FORWARD LIMIT

SEATBACK FRONTAL SURFACE PLANE EXTENDED

UPPER RESTRAINT SURFACE POINT

90°

UPPER LIMIT

VERTICAL REFERENCE LINE

90°

70° MAXIMUM DURING IMPACT

NOTE: Limits illustrated move during dynamic testing

---

[12] Both the current FMVSS No. 213 and the 213 Final Rule published June 24, 2003 have identical criteria for seat back rotation

Table 3

Base vs. No Base				
Restraint	*Seat Rotation (in degrees)*		HIC_{36}	
	Base	*No Base*	*Base*	*No Base*
Cosco Eddie Bauer Infant Seat	60	49	536	343
Evenflo Portabout 5	N/A	62	436	412
Evenflo Portabout 3	60	68	486	470
Graco Snugride	59	46	654	181
Cosco Designer 22 5-pt.	54	53	425	259
Evenflo Discovery	64	58	469	229

The agency also observed differences in the bottom contour for some of the restraints with and without their base, as well as differences in the belt path between the two configurations. The coupling between the infant restraint and its base may also be a factor, leading to a great discontinuity between the sled bench and the CRABI dummy. However, due to measurement limitations, it is difficult to quantify how large a role all of these factors may have played in the overall difference in performance between the two configurations.

One child restraint would have failed the FMVSS No. 213 compliance test[13] because the seat completely released from the base during the test[14,15]. Therefore, it was not possible to measure the seat rotation for this test. However, the injury values for both HIC and chest acceleration were well below the IARVs and consistent with other infant seats tested in this series. It is likely that the agency did not see a high HIC or chest acceleration value for this restraint because the upper portion of the seat did not travel a great distance away from the base, nor did it contact any other objects during the event.

Although there was a slight performance difference between the two configurations, it is important to note that NHTSA believes use of the removable base

---

[13] Final Rule published June 24, 2003
[14] Evenflo Portabout 5 with base attachment model # 3861352P1
[15] The Office of Enforcement was informed of the occurrence.

provides several desirable design features for consumers (i.e., ease of installation) therefore the agency is not suggesting that consumers stop using the removable base with these infant restraints. Furthermore, in every case, both with and without the removable base attached to the infant restraint, the CRABI dummy sustained HIC and chest acceleration values that were well below the normalized IARV values.

C) 3YO vs. CRABI Rear-Facing:

The third test series analyzed seven pairs of convertible restraints in the rear-facing position with both a Hybrid III 3YO dummy and a CRABI dummy. These restraints were again secured using lower anchorages. The variable in this series of tests was the different test dummy. Four different child restraint manufacturers were represented in this group of tests. The agency tested convertible restraints with 5-point harnesses and overhead shields with 3-point harnesses, but for this series of tests their performances were not compared. The results showed a statistical difference in HIC between the 3YO dummy and CRABI dummy for these tests, with the CRABI having a lower HIC.[16] Figure 10 shows the HIC results obtained in this series. There was no statistical difference between the chest acceleration values for the CRABI and 3YO dummies and these values can be seen in Figure 11.

---

[16] Statistical difference at the 95% confidence interval (.05 level)

Figure 10

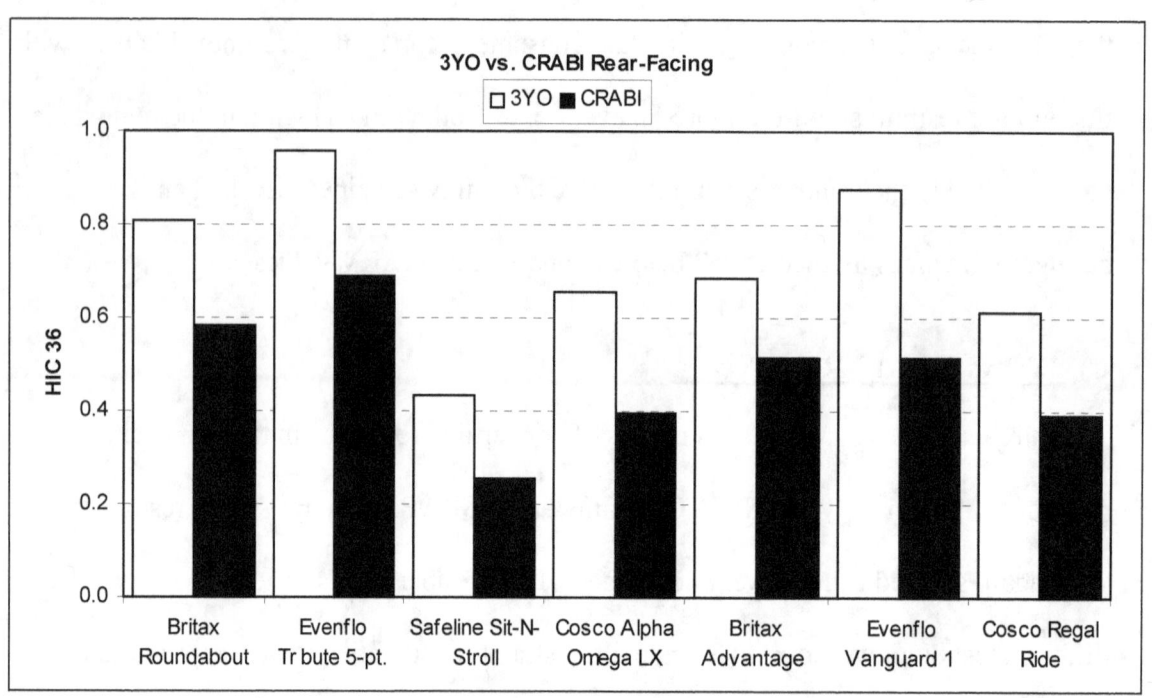

Figure 11

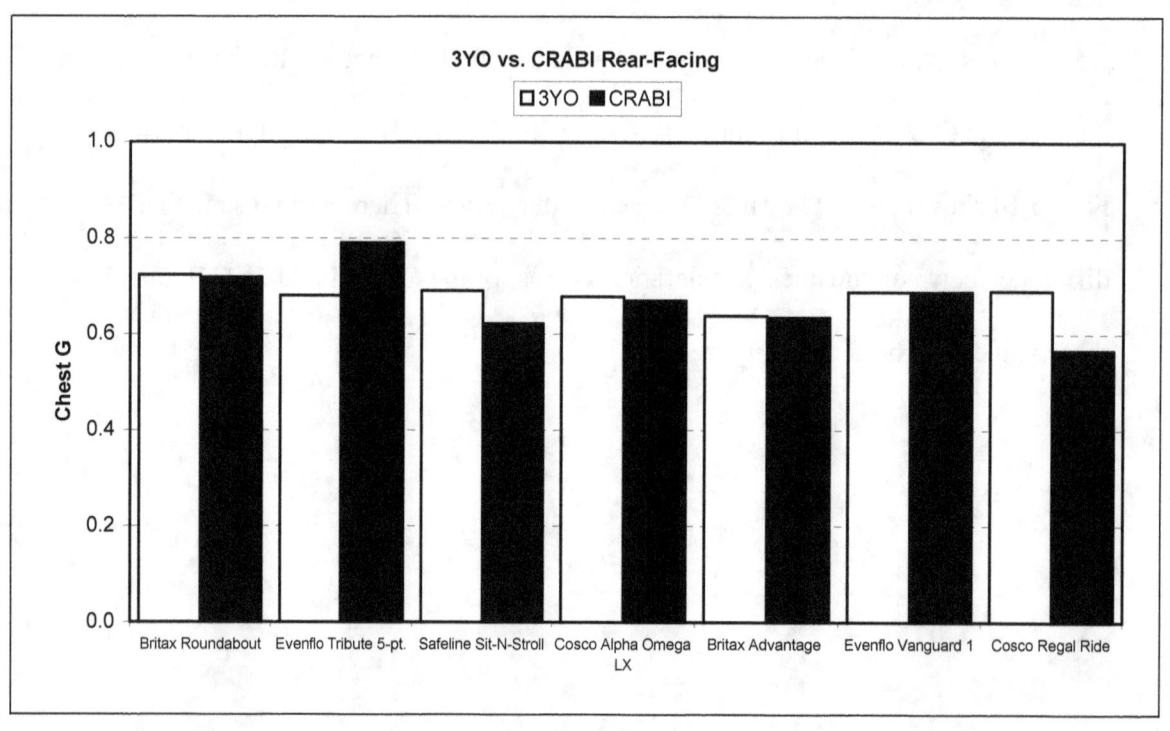

As mentioned in the previous section, the agency did not collect head or knee excursion measurements for rear-facing tests; however, the rotation angle of the seat back was measured for each child restraint. Again, the agency observed lower seat rotation angles for the seats that had lower HIC numbers in all except for one case. Table 4 lists the seat back rotation angles for the seven restraints tested with the 3YO and CRABI dummies. For the one case where the Hybrid III 3YO had a lower seat rotation angle, the difference in rotation was only one degree. These larger seat rotations often result in a larger "z" component of the HIC calculation and an overall greater head rotation during the event, which may likely increase the HIC values. Figure 12 shows the larger head "z" component for the 3YO dummy. This same trend can be seen in the other six restraints tested in this series as well.

Figure 12
Britax Roundabout

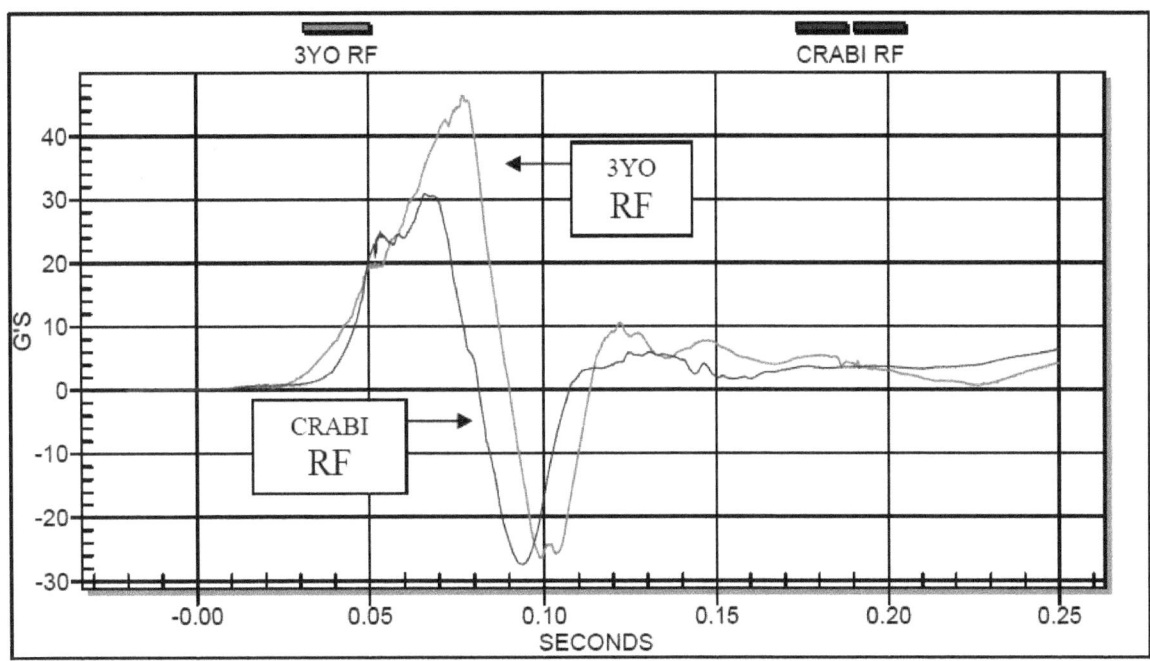

The physical differences between the two dummies likely causes the different seatback rotation angles. The 3YO dummy has a significantly heavier upper body, which results in a greater total weight above the pivot point in the CRS. Table 5 provides the segment and full assembly weight of the CRABI dummy and the Hybrid III 3YO.

Table 4

3 YO vs. CRABI Rear Facing					
		Seat Rotation (in degrees)		HIC_{36}	
Restraint	Type	3YO	CRABI	3YO	CRABI
Britax Roundabout	Convertible	54	43	807	584
Evenflo Tribute 5-pt.	Convertible	45	46	957*	691
Safeline Sit-N-Stroll	Convertible	36	34	435	256
Cosco Alpha Omega LX	Combination	58	52	655	396
Britax Advantage	Convertible	51	45	687	517
Evenflo Vanguard 5	Convertible	52	50	878	516
Cosco Regal Ride	Convertible	68	57	613	393

*Head to Feet contact

Table 5

Dummy	CRABI 12-Month-Old	Hybrid III 3-Year-Old
Part	Weight (lb.)	Weight (lb.)
Head	5.79	5.92
Neck	0.84	1.65
Torso	8.11	14.42
Arms (2)	2.64	3.96
Legs (2)	4.62	8.14
Total	22.00	34.09

D) 3YO vs. CRABI Forward-Facing

The next series tested seven child restraint models in the forward-facing position with both the HYBRID III 3YO dummy and the CRABI dummy. The agency tested both combination and convertible restraints, as well as 5-point harnesses and overhead shields (with a 3 pt. harness) in this round of tests. Two of the combination seats tested were designed for use as a rear-facing and forward-facing convertible restraint as well as a belt-positioning booster seat. One of these restraints was an overhead shield and the other was a 5-point harness. The other two combination seats were designed for use as rear-facing and forward-facing convertible restraint. Again, one of the combination seats was an overhead shield model and the other was a 5-point harness. All child restraints in this test series were secured using LATCH. The test results indicated that the dynamic performance of the forward-facing child restraint was independent of the dummy type. The differences in HIC and chest acceleration between the CRABI and 3YO dummies were not statistically significant. These HIC and chest acceleration data can be seen in Figures 13 and 14 respectively. The agency did not find any statistical difference for head or knee excursion measurements for the 3YO and CRABI dummies either. This data is shown in Table 6.

Table 6

3 YO vs. CRABI Forward Facing					
Restraint	Type	Head Excursion* (mm)		Knee Excursion** (mm)	
		3YO	CRABI	3YO	CRABI
Cosco Touriva 5-pt.	Convertible	551	472	604	462
Cosco Touriva OHS	Convertible	523	437	640	503
Cosco Alpha Omega 5-pt.	Combination	604	490	681	546
Cosco Alpha Omega OHS	Combination	678	452	711	536
Evenflo Titan V	Convertible	572	480	656	503
Graco Comfort Sport	Convertible	551	442	637	500
Graco Comfort Sport 2 in 1	Convertible	610	551	770	559

*FMVSS No. 213 Head Excursion limit: 720 mm with top tether, 813 mm without top tether
**FMVSS No. 213 Knee Excursion limit: 914 mm

Figure 13

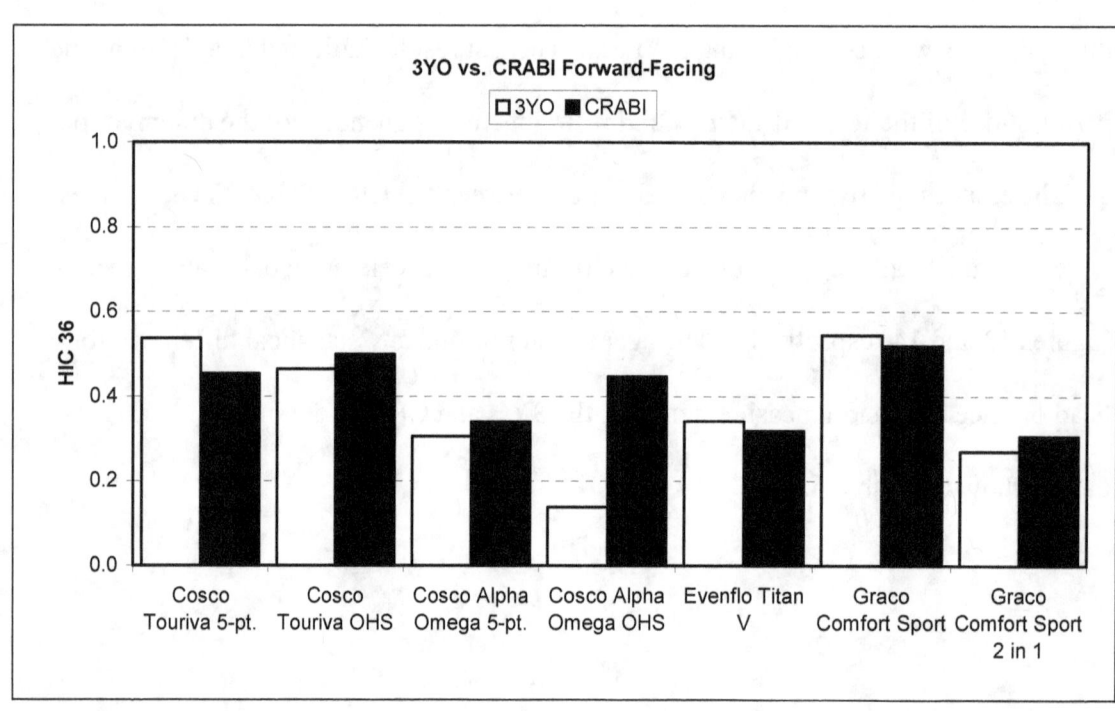

Figure 14

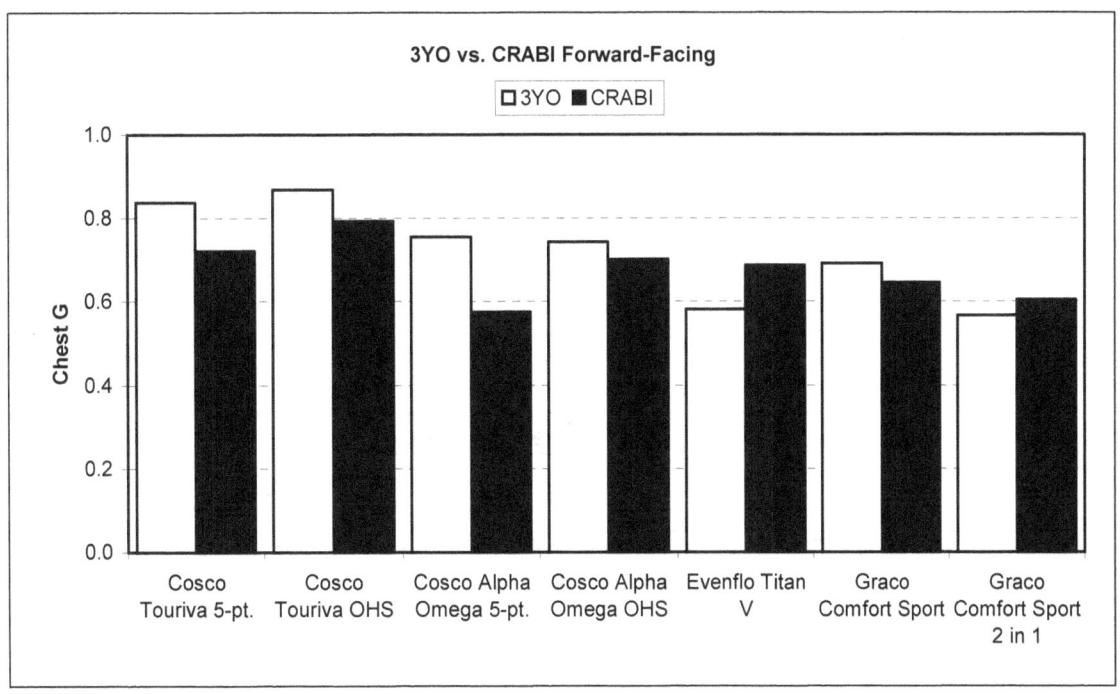

E) LATCH vs. Lap Belt w/ Top Tether

In the notice published November of 2001[17], the agency stated that both LATCH

and lap belt with top tether had similar performance; however, the sample size was

limited due to the number of CRS on the market at the time that were equipped with

LATCH. Therefore, the agency decided to conduct additional tests on this issue. The

anchorage points remained in the same location for these tests in order to simulate the

center seating position and the lap belt tests were performed in the center seating

position. These additional tests included four combination child restraints and four

convertible child restraints. Each child restraint was tested in the forward facing position

with the Hybrid III 3YO dummy. The additional tests confirmed the 2001 findings,

showing no statistical difference in performance between the Hybrid III 3YO dummy in a

---

[17] 66 FR 56146 (Docket No. NHTSA-2001-10053-Notice 1)

forward-facing restraint with LATCH and the Hybrid III 3YO dummy in a forward-facing restraint with lap belt and top tether. The HIC values for both the LATCH and lap belt with top tether configurations are shown in Figure 15, and the chest acceleration values for these two configurations are shown in Figure 16. Head and knee excursions are provided in Table 7.

Table 7

LATCH vs. Lap Belt/Tether					
Restraint	Type	Head Excursion* (mm)		Knee Excursion** (mm)	
		LATCH	Lap Belt/Tether	LATCH	Lap Belt/Tether
Britax Expressway ISOFIX	Convertible	546	584	544	640
Britax Husky Marina	Convertible	544	556	673	686
Graco Ultra Cargo	Combination	594	612	589	686
Cosco Eddie Bauer Hi-Back	Combination	645	627	643	790
Evenflo Triumph 5	Convertible	496	495	602	729
Safety First Comfort Ride	Convertible	640	655	604	698
Evenflo Victory 5	Convertible	577	643	663	764
Evenflo Vanguard 1	Convertible	594	622	643	747

*FMVSS No. 213 Head Excursion limit: 720 mm with top tether, 813 mm without top tether
**FMVSS No. 213 Knee Excursion limit: 914 mm

Figure 15

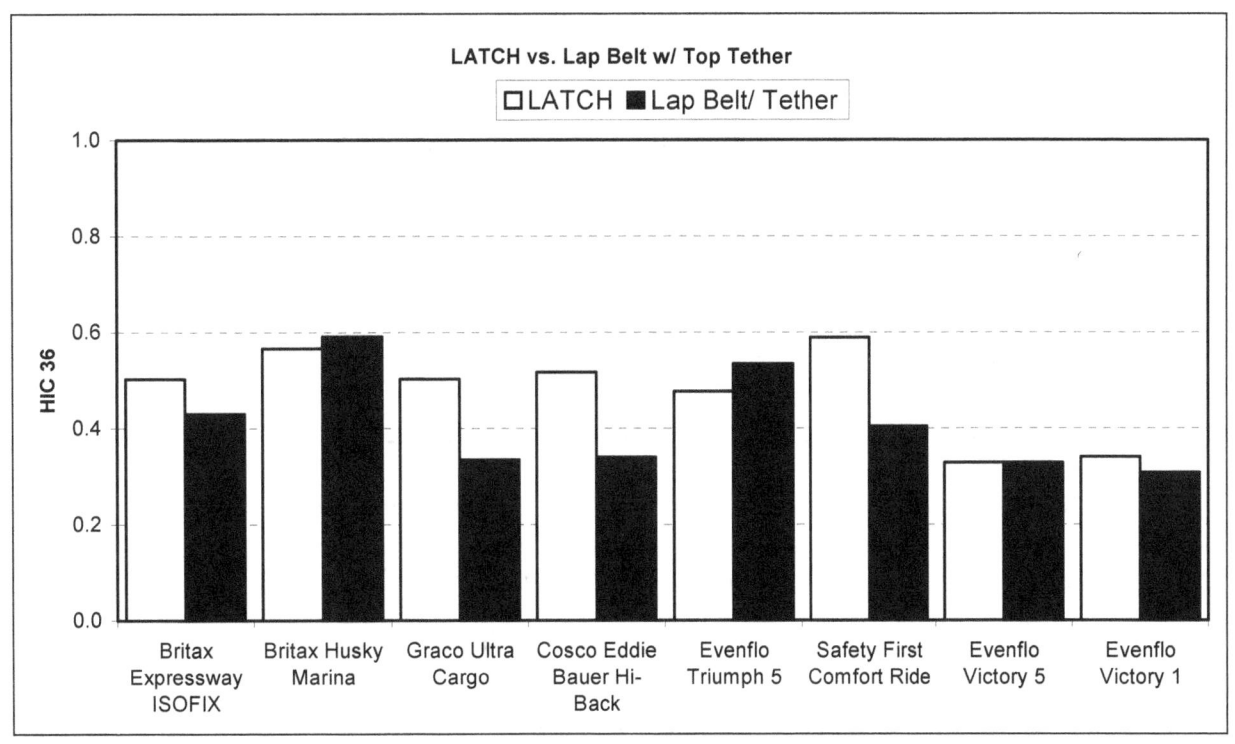

Figure 16

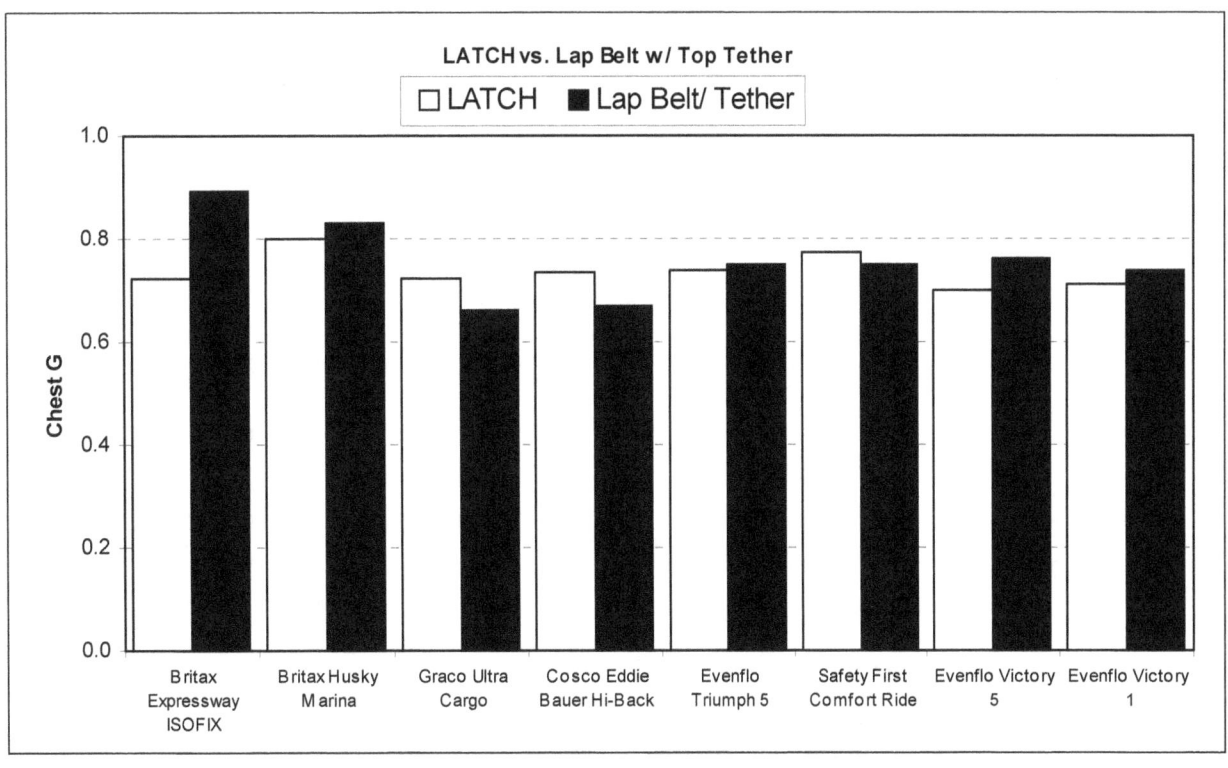

F) <u>HYBRID III 3YO vs. HYBRID III 6YO in Belt-Positioning Booster w/ 3pt. Belt</u>

The final series of tests considered the Hybrid III 3YO dummy and the Hybrid III 6YO dummy in the belt-positioning booster. Although children significantly older than 3 years of age usually use belt-positioning boosters, many of these booster seats have minimum weight specifications that allow the 3YO dummy to be used. Eight high back belt-positioning booster seats were tested with both the Hybrid III 3YO and Hybrid III 6YO dummies. The dummy type was the variable of interest in this series of tests. Six different child seat manufacturers were represented in these tests and each booster seat was tested in one of the two outboard positions on the sled bench with a 3-point belt. The outboard seating positions of the sled bench were changed back to their original specifications for this test series. The results show that the HIC values for the Hybrid III 3YO dummy are statistically higher than the Hybrid III 6YO dummy.[18] The HIC values are shown in Figure 17. The difference in chest acceleration between the two configurations was small and not statistically significant (see Figure 18). Head and knee excursions can be found in Table 8.

---

[18] Statistical difference at the 95% confidence interval (.05 level)

Figure 17

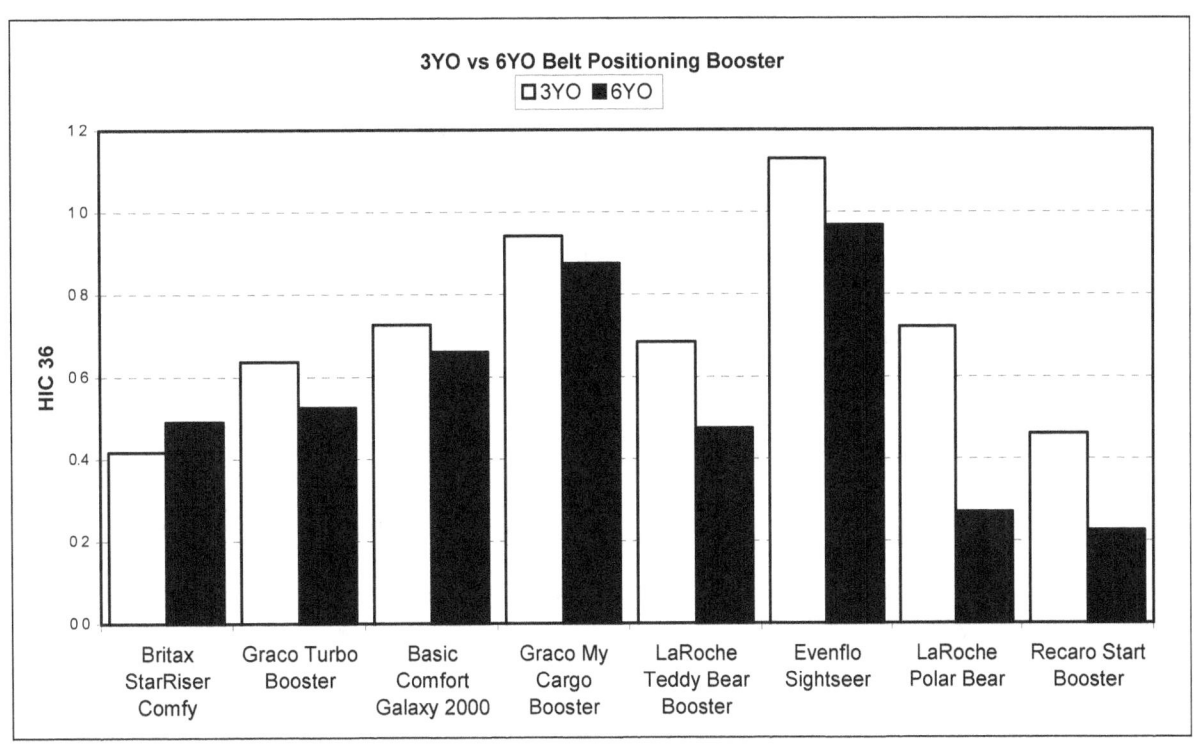

Figure 18

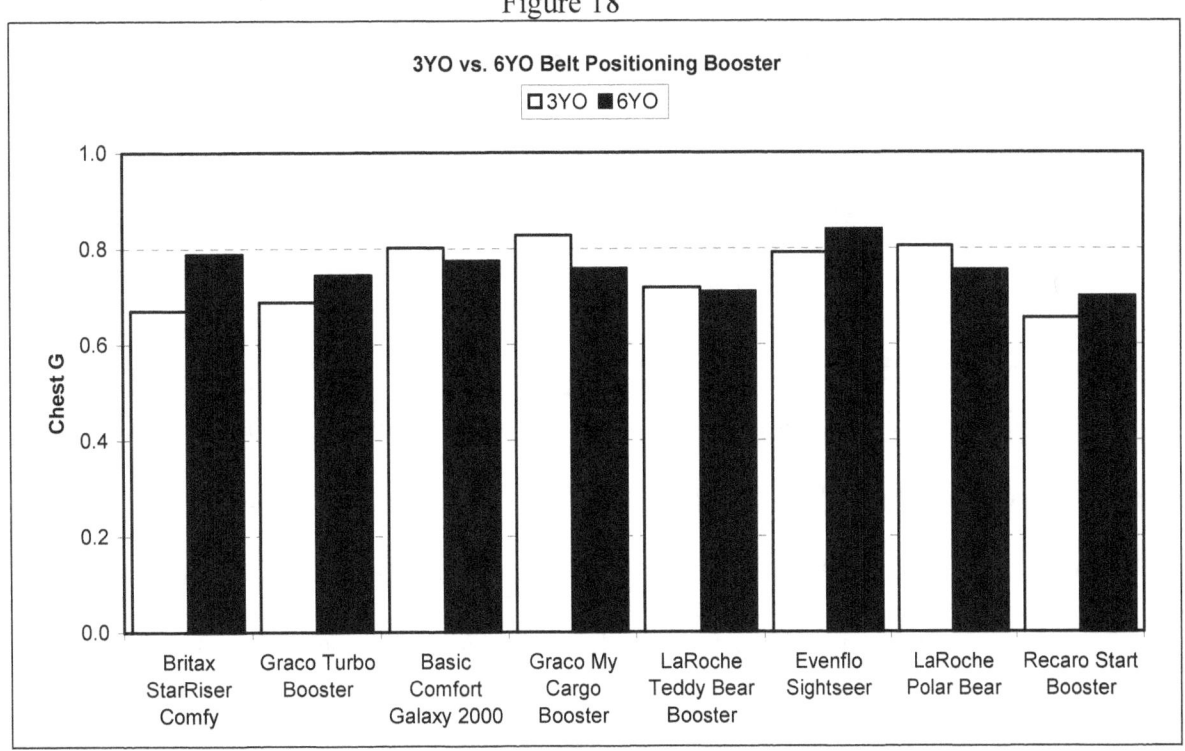

27

Table 8

3 YO vs. 6 YO Belt Positioning Booster 3-pt. Belt				
	Head Excursion* (mm)		Knee Excursion** (mm)	
Restraint	3YO	6YO	3YO	6YO
Britax StarRiser Comfy	483	516	483	549
Graco Turbo Booster	467	472	533	566
Basic Comfort Galaxy 2000	483	483	528	564
Graco My Cargo Booster	485	490	523	579
LaRoache Teddy Bear Booster	452	457	521	574
Evenflo Sightseer	498	510	617	645
LaRoche Polar Bear	467	475	551	597
Recaro Start Booster	508	551	528	579

*FMVSS No. 213 Head Excursion limit: 720 mm with top tether, 813 mm without top tether
**FMVSS No. 213 Knee Excursion limit: 914 mm

A likely reason for the different dynamic performances between the two configurations is the physical differences between the two dummies. Film analysis shows noticeably different kinematic responses between the 3YO and 6YO in the head and neck region. The 6YO dummy tends to have greater head rotation as well as a longer duration of rotation during the event which likely accounts for some part of the lower HIC values. Table 9 shows the head and knee excursions for the 3YO and 6YO dummies in the different belt-positioning boosters tested in this series. This set of tests had the only child restraint that exceeded a maximum HIC value of 1000.[19]

G)   Dynamic Performance Range

The second goal for the FY 2003 testing was to determine the range of dynamic performances between CRS models of the same type, secured in the same configuration, and with the same dummy. The six test series discussed above did not directly address the range of child seat performance based upon different child seat models. While the same child seat model was used within each pair to control for any performance

_____

[19] Evenflo Sightseer with 3YO model # 2692198P1

28

differences across models, a variety of different child seat models were used in each test series. Choosing a variety of seats increases the ability to apply the results across a variety of child seat models. Questions about the range of performance across models can be addressed by comparing the results of various models with the same configuration and dummy across the sled tests. Previous testing performed by the agency has shown the repeatability of the FMVSS No. 213 sled test, allowing the agency to assume that the variation across sled tests is a much smaller component of the total variation than the variation due to different child seat models.[20] This assumption was necessary when determining the range of dynamic performances between different CRS models, because unlike the previous analysis, the child restraints being compared were not always tested on the same sled run.

The range of performance is described using deciles. Deciles divide the distribution of the FMVSS No. 213 IARVs into 10 groups having equal frequencies, or in other words every 10 percent using the HIC limit of 1000 and chest acceleration limit of 60. The graphs below show the range of performance for three different dummies restrained in their typical child seat type and configurations. The first graph, Figure 20, shows the range of dynamic performance for the 3YO dummy in either a convertible or combination seat in the forward-facing position. The second graph, Figure 21, shows the dynamic performance range for the CRABI dummy secured in an infant seat in the rear-facing position. The third graph, Figure 22, shows the dynamic performance range for the 6YO dummy forward-facing in a belt-positioning booster seat.

---

[20] Docket No. NHTSA-03-15351-4

Figure 20

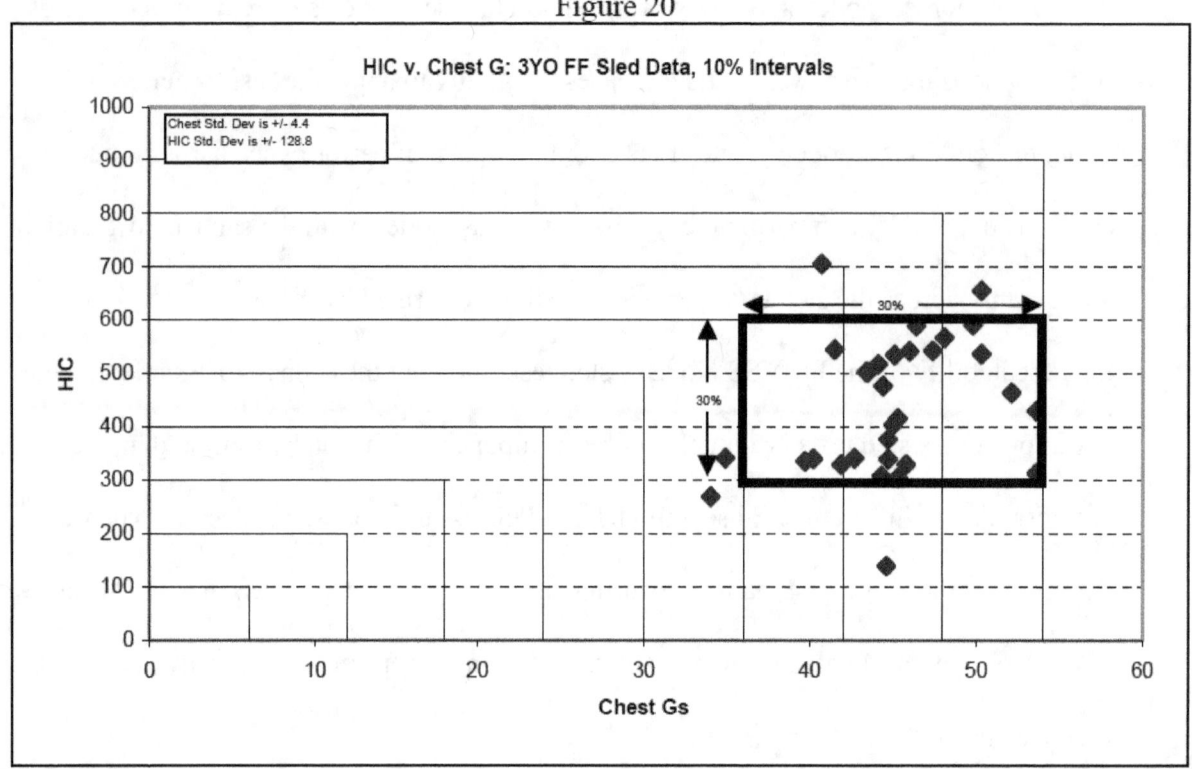

Figure 21

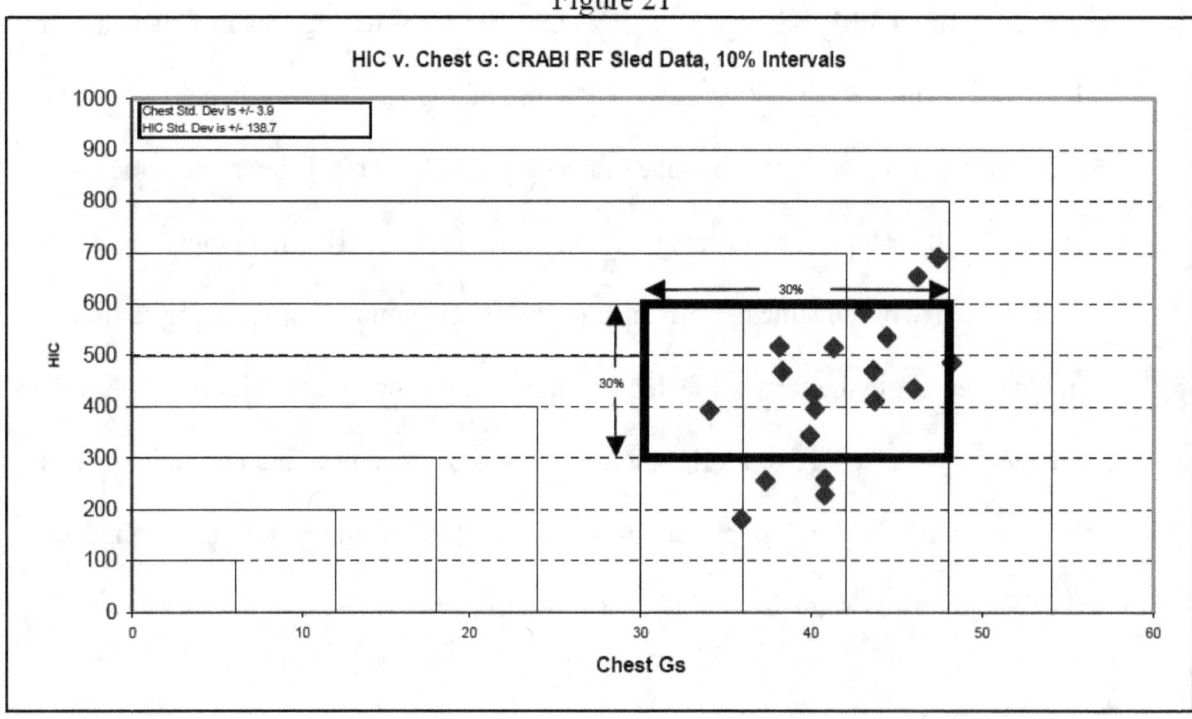

Figure 22

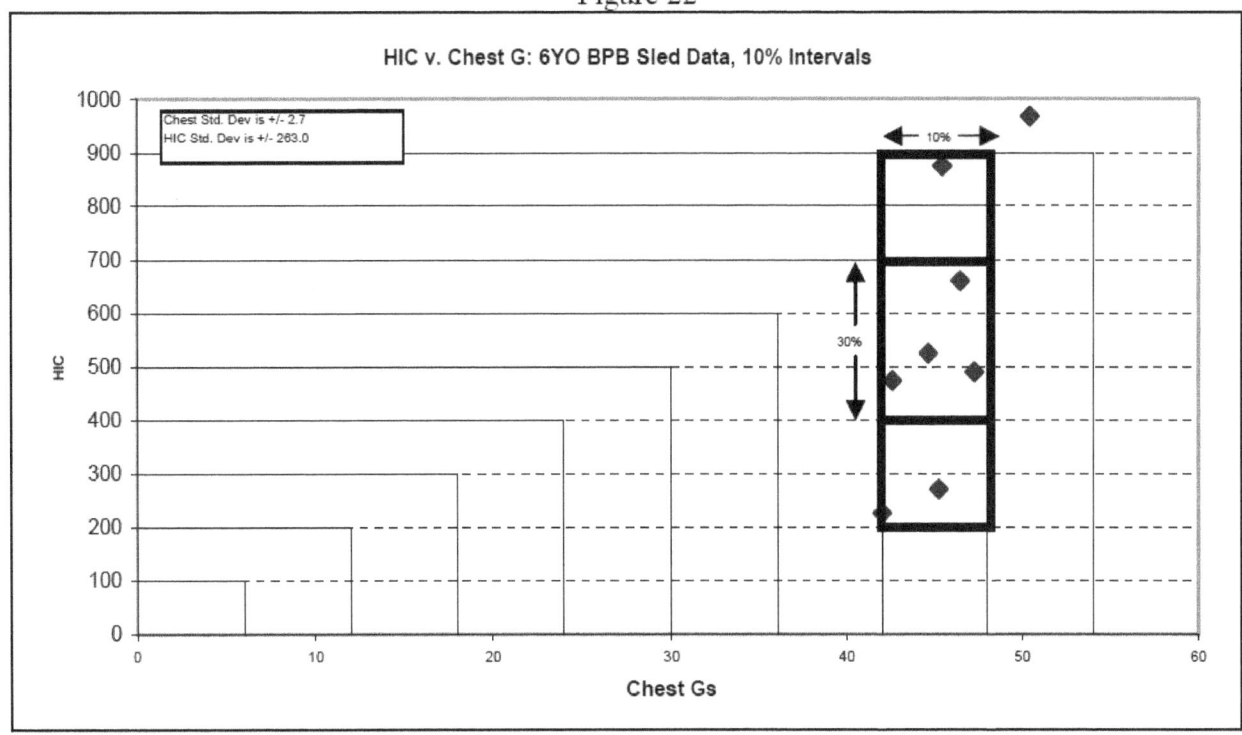

The testing performed also confirmed earlier studies done by the agency showing relatively small dynamic performance differences for HIC and chest acceleration between different CRS models tested on the sled in the same configuration.[21] In fact, 26 of the 31 convertible/combination child restraints in the forward-facing position fell within an interval that is 30% of the FMVSS No. 213 IARVs. Similar results were seen for the CRABI rear-facing where 13 of 19 infant restraints in the rear-facing position fell within a 30% interval of the FMVSS No. 213 IARVs. All but one belt-positioning booster seat fell within an interval that is 10% of the FMVSS No. 213 IARVs, however, the HIC values were more varied resulting in only half of the booster seats being within an interval that is 30% of FMVSS No. 213 IARVs. Nevertheless, none of the child restraints

---

[21] In the November 5, 2002 notice (67 FR 514 Docket No. NHTSA-2001-10053), the agency stated that sled testing showed similar performance between different CRS model, as such, all child restraints subjected to the sled test would have received either a four- or five-star rating.

exceeded the HIC or chest acceleration FMVSS No. 213 IARV limits of HIC of 1000 and chest G of 60

Due to the large number and variety of child restraints tested, the agency has sufficient reason to believe that this is good indication of the range of dynamic performances the agency would expect to find for all current child restraint models sold on the market.

V. <u>CONCLUSIONS</u>:

The sled tests discussed in this report provided the agency with significant new information and data and, more importantly, were successful in resolving many unanswered questions and issues that have previously been raised. Several deductions can be drawn from this testing:

- There were no statistical differences in injury values accrued between:
    1. One vs. two child restraints on the sled bench
    2. The CRABI and 3YO in the same forward-facing convertible or combination seat
    3. The 3YO in the same convertible or combination CRS secured with either LATCH or lap belt with top tether

- There were statistical differences in HIC performance for:

  1. The CRABI dummy in the base vs. no base test series

  2. The CRABI and 3YO dummy in the same rear-facing convertible or combination restraint

  3. The 3YO and 6YO dummy in the same Belt-positioning booster

- The agency cannot assume similar HIC or chest acceleration results for the same CRS model in different configurations independent of dummy type.

- The agency found that for any given configuration, many makes and models were within an interval of 30% of the FMVSS No. 213 IARVs for HIC and chest acceleration. This included the convertible and combination restraints as well as the infant restraints, and belt-positioning booster seats. This indicates a relatively small spread in HIC and chest acceleration for the same child restraint type in the same configuration, regardless of child restraint make or model. Additionally, most all of the child restraints injury values fell well under the HIC limit of 1000 and Chest acceleration limit of 60.

VI. APPENDIX A:

TABLE A-1 All Sled Test Results

TST NO	MODEL	DUM TYP	DUM SIZE	OCC LOC	HIC	CLIP 3M	CONFIG	HEAD EXC	KNEE EXC	ROT
4787	COSCO SUMMIT	H3	3YO	6	415	45.3	FF	561	701	N/A
4788	EVENFLO EXPRESS	H3	3YO	6	542	47.4	FF	503	635	N/A
4789	CENTURY 1500 STE	H3	3YO	6	655	50.3	FF	572	645	N/A
4790	BRITAX MARATHON	H3	3YO	6	377	44.7	FF	551	650	N/A
4791	COSCO SUMMIT	H3	3YO	3	339	44.7	FF	572	678	N/A
4791	EVENFLO EXPRESS	H3	3YO	4	542	46	FF	513	671	N/A
4792	CENTURY 1500 STE	H3	3YO	3	706	40.7	FF	551	660	N/A
4792	BRITAX MARATHON	H3	3YO	4	312	53.6	FF	417	594	N/A
4793	COSCO EDDIE BAUER WITH BASE	CR	1YO	3	536	44.4	RF	N/A	N/A	60
4793	COSCO EDDIE BAUER WITHOUT BASE	CR	1YO	4	343	39.9	RF	N/A	N/A	49
4794	EVENFLO PORTABOUT 5 WITH BASE	CR	1YO	3	435	46	RF	N/A	N/A	N/A
4794	EVENFLO PORTABOUT 5 WITHOUT BASE	CR	1YO	4	411	43.7	RF	N/A	N/A	62
4795	EVENFLO PORTABOUT 3 WITH BASE	CR	1YO	3	484	48.2	RF	N/A	N/A	60
4795	EVENFLO PORTABOUT 3 WITHOUT BASE	CR	1YO	4	469	43.5	RF	N/A	N/A	68
4796	GRACO SNUGRIDE WITH BASE	CR	1YO	3	653	46.1	RF	N/A	N/A	59
4796	GRACO SNUGRIDE WITHOUT BASE	CR	1YO	4	180	35.8	RF	N/A	N/A	46
4800	BRITAX ROUNDABOUT	H3	3YO	3	806	43.4	RF	N/A	N/A	54
4800	BRITAX ROUNDABOUT	CR	1YO	4	583	43.1	RF	N/A	N/A	43
4801	EVENFLO TRIBUTE 5 POINT	H3	3YO	3	957	40.8	RF	N/A	N/A	45
4801	EVENFLO TRIBUTE 5 POINT	CR	1YO	4	691	47.4	RF	N/A	N/A	46
4802	SAFELINE SIT-N-STROLL	H3	3YO	3	434	41.3	RF	N/A	N/A	36

34

ID	Name						RF/FF			34
4802	SAFELINE SIT-N-STROLL	CR	1YO	4	256	37.3	RF	N/A	N/A	34
4803	COSCO TOURIVA 5 POINT	H3	3YO	3	536	50.3	FF	551	604	N/A
4803	COSCO TOURIVA 5 POINT	CR	1YO	4	454	43.3	FF	472	462	N/A
4804	COSCO TOURIVA OHS	H3	3YO	3	464	52.1	FF	523	640	N/A
4804	COSCO TOURIVA OHS	CR	1YO	4	500	47.6	FF	437	503	N/A
4805	COSCO ALPHA OMEGA	H3	3YO	3	304	45.3	FF	604	681	N/A
4805	COSCO ALPHA OMEGA	CR	1YO	4	338	34.5	FF	490	546	N/A
4806	COSCO ALPHA OMEGA OHS	H3	3YO	3	139	44.6	FF	678	711	N/A
4806	COSCO ALPHA OMEGA OHS	CR	1YO	4	447	42.1	FF	452	536	N/A
4807	EVENFLO TITAN V	H3	3YO	3	341	34.9	FF	572	656	N/A
4807	EVENFLO TITAN V	CR	1YO	4	317	41.2	FF	480	503	N/A
4808	GRACO COMFORT SPORT	H3	3YO	3	544	41.5	FF	551	637	N/A
4808	GRACO COMFORT SPORT	CR	1YO	4	519	38.6	FF	442	500	N/A
4811	BRITAX EXPRESSWAY ISOFIX WITH LATCH	H3	3YO	3	503	43.5	FF	546	544	N/A
4811	BRITAX HUSKY MARINA WITH LATCH	H3	3YO	4	566	48.1	FF	544	673	N/A
4812	GRACO ULTRA CARGO WITH LATCH	H3	3YO	3	502	43.3	FF	594	589	N/A
4812	COSCO EDDIE BAUER HI-BACK WITH LATCH	H3	3YO	4	516	44.1	FF	645	643	N/A
4813	EVENFLO TRIUMPH 5 WITH LATCH	H3	3YO	3	476	44.3	FF	496	602	N/A
4813	SAFETY FIRST COMFORT RIDE WITH LATCH	H3	3YO	4	589	46.4	FF	640	604	N/A
4814	EVENFLO VICTORY 5 WITH LATCH	H3	3YO	3	328	41.9	FF	577	663	N/A
4814	EVENFLO VANGUARD 1 WITH LATCH	H3	3YO	4	341	42.7	FF	594	643	N/A
4815	BRITAX EXPRESSWAY ISOFIX WITH LAP BELT / TOP TETHER	H3	3YO	6	430	53.6	FF	584	640	N/A
4816	BRITAX HUSKY MARINA WITH LAP BELT / TOP TETHER	H3	3YO	6	591	49.8	FF	556	686	N/A
4817	GRACO ULTRA CARGO WITH LAP BELT / TOP TETHER	H3	3YO	6	334	39.7	FF	612	686	N/A
4818	EVENFLO VICTORY 5 WITH LAP BELT / TOP TETHER	H3	3YO	6	328	45.8	FF	643	764	N/A
4819	EVENFLO VANGUARD 1 WITH LAP BELT / TOP TETHER	H3	3YO	6	308	44.3	FF	622	747	N/A
4831	BRITAX STARRISER COMFY	H3	3YO	3	416	40.2	FF	483	483	N/A
4831	BRITAX STARRISER COMFY	H3	6YO	4	489	47.3	FF	516	549	N/A
4832	GRACO TURBO BOOSTER	H3	3YO	3	636	41.3	FF	467	533	N/A
4832	GRACO TURBO BOOSTER	H3	6YO	4	525	44.6	FF	472	566	N/A
4833	BASIC COMFORT GALAXIE 2000	H3	3YO	3	726	48	FF	483	528	N/A
4833	BASIC COMFORT GALAXIE 2000	H3	6YO	4	659	46.4	FF	483	564	N/A

ID	Product	Type	Age				Dir			
4834	GRACO MY CARGO BOOSTER	H3	3YO	3	941	49.6	FF	485	523	N/A
4834	GRACO MY CARGO BOOSTER	H3	6YO	4	874	45.5	FF	490	579	N/A
4835	LAROCHE TEDDY BEAR BOOSTER	H3	3YO	3	683	43	FF	452	521	N/A
4835	LAROCHE TEDDY BEAR BOOSTER	H3	6YO	4	473	42.6	FF	457	574	N/A
4836	EVENFLO SIGHTSEER	H3	3YO	3	1130	47.4	FF	498	617	N/A
4836	EVENFLO SIGHTSEER	H3	6YO	4	967	50.3	FF	510	645	N/A
4839	COSCO ALPHA OMEGA LX	H3	3YO	3	654	40.7	RF	N/A	N/A	58
4839	COSCO ALPHA OMEGA LX	CR	1YO	4	396	40.1	RF	N/A	N/A	52
4840	BRITAX ADVANTAGE	H3	3YO	3	688	38.2	RF	N/A	N/A	51
4840	BRITAX ADVANTAGE	CR	1YO	4	516	38.1	RF	N/A	N/A	45
4841	EVENFLO VANGARD 5	H3	3YO	3	877	41.3	RF	N/A	N/A	52
4841	EVENFLO VANGARD 5	H3	1YO	4	516	41.3	RF	N/A	N/A	50
4842	COSCO DESIGNER 22 5-PT WITH BASE	CR	1YO	3	424	40.1	RF	N/A	N/A	54
4842	COSCO DESIGNER 22 5-PT WITHOUT BASE	CR	1YO	4	257	40.8	RF	N/A	N/A	53
4843	EVENFLO DISCOVERY WITH BASE	CR	1YO	3	469	38.3	RF	N/A	N/A	64
4843	EVENFLO DISCOVERY WITHOUT BASE	CR	1YO	4	228	40.7	RF	N/A	N/A	58
4844	COSCO REGAL RIDE	CH	3YO	3	612	41.3	RF	N/A	N/A	68
4844	COSCO REGAL RIDE	CR	1YO	4	392	33.9	RF	N/A	N/A	57
4845	GRACO COMFORTSPORT 2 IN 1	CH	3YO	3	268	34	FF	610	770	N/A
4845	GRACO COMFORTSPORT 2 IN 1	CR	1YO	4	305	36.3	FF	551	559	N/A
4847	DOREL EDDIE BAUER HB WITH LAP BELT / TOP TETHER	H3	3YO	6	340	40.2	FF	627	790	N/A
4848	EVENFLO TRIUMPH 5 WITH LAP BELT / TOP TETHER	H3	3YO	6	534	45.1	FF	495	729	N/A
4849	SAFETY FIRST COMFORT RIDE	H3	3YO	6	403	45	FF	655	698	N/A
4850	LAROCHE POLAR BEAR BOOSTER	H3	3YO	3	720	48.2	FF	467	551	N/A
4850	LAROCHE POLAR BEAR BOOSTER	H3	6YO	4	269	45.3	FF	475	597	N/A
4851	RECARO START BOOSTER	H3	3YO	3	460	39.2	FF	508	528	N/A
4851	RECARO START BOOSTER	H3	6YO	4	224	41.9	FF	551	579	N/A

TABLE A-2 Test Series

One CRS w/ 3YO Forward-Facing vs. Two CRS w/ 3YO Forward-Facing				
	HIC36		Chest G	
Restraint	One	Two	One	Two
Cosco Summit	416	339	45.3	44.7
Evenflo Express	543	542	47.4	46.0
Century 1500 STE	656	706	50.3	40.7
Britax Marathon	377	313	44.7	53.6

Base with CRABI Rear-Facing vs. No Base with CRABI Rear-Facing				
	HIC36		Chest G	
Restraint	Base	No Base	Base	No Base
Cosco Eddie Bauer Infant Seat	536	343	44.4	39.9
Evenflo Portabout 5	436	412	46.0	43.7
Evenflo Portabout 3	486	470	48.2	43.6
Graco Snugride	654	181	46.2	35.9
Cosco Designer 22 5-pt.	425	259	40.1	40.8
Evenflo Discovery	469	229	38.3	40.8

3 YO Rear-Facing vs. CRABI Rear-Facing				
	HIC36		Chest G	
Restraint	3YO	CRABI	3YO	CRABI
Britax Roundabout	807	584	43.4	43.1
Evenflo Tribute 5-pt.	957	691	40.8	47.4
Safeline Sit-N-Stroll	435	256	41.4	37.3
Cosco Alpha Omega LX	655	396	40.7	40.2
Britax Advantage	687	517	38.3	38.1
Evenflo Vanguard 5	878	516	41.3	41.3
Cosco Regal Ride	613	393	41.4	34.0

3 YO Forward-Facing vs. CRABI Forward-Facing				
	HIC36		Chest G	
Restraint	3YO	CRABI	3YO	CRABI
Cosco Touriva 5-pt.	537	454	50.3	43.3
Cosco Touriva OHS	464	500	52.1	47.6
Cosco Alpha Omega 5-pt.	305	339	45.3	34.5
Cosco Alpha Omega OHS	139	447	44.6	42.1
Evenflo Titan V	341	318	34.9	41.2
Graco Comfort Sport	545	520	41.5	38.7
Graco Comfort Sport 2 in 1	269	305	34.0	36.3

LATCH with 3YO Forward-Facing vs. Lap Belt/ Top Tether with 3YO Forward-Facing				
	HIC36		Chest G	
Restraint	LATCH	Lap Belt/Tether	LATCH	Lap Belt/Tether
Britax Expressway ISOFIX	503	430	43.5	53.6
Britax Husky Marina	567	591	48.1	49.8
Graco Ultra Cargo	503	335	43.4	39.7
Cosco Eddie Bauer Hi-Back	517	340	44.1	40.2

Evenflo Triumph 5	477	535	44.4	45.1
Safety First Comfort Ride	589	404	46.4	45.0
Evenflo Victory 5	329	329	41.9	45.8
Evenflo Victory 1	341	308	42.7	44.3

3 YO in Belt-Positioning Booster w/ 3 pt. belt vs. 6 YO Belt-Positioning Booster w/3-pt. Belt

Restraint	HIC36		Chest G	
	3YO	6YO	3YO	6YO
Britax StarRiser Comfy	417	490	40.2	47.3
Graco Turbo Booster	637	525	41.3	44.7
Basic Comfort Galaxy 2000	727	660	48.1	46.5
Graco My Cargo Booster	943	875	49.7	45.5
LaRoache Teddy Bear Booster	684	474	43.1	42.6
Evenflo Sightseer	1130	968	47.5	50.4
LaRoache Polar Bear	721	271	48.3	45.3
Recaro Start Booster	461	226	39.3	42.0

TABLE A-3 t-Tests Results

	HIC	Chest G
1 CRS on Sled vs. Two	0.4918	0.8698
Base vs. No Base	0.0426	0.1562
3YO vs. CRABI RF	0.0001	0.6220
3YO vs. CRABI FF	0.4284	0.2528
LATCH vs. Belt w/ Top Tether	0.0830	0.8921
3YO vs. 6YO BPB	0.0254	0.5475

TABLE A-4 Standard Deviations

	3YO FF w/ LATCH	3YO FF	6YO in BPB	CRABI RF
Chest G Mean	44.55	44.9483871	45.5375	41.5
Chest G Std. Dev.	4.670257418	4.423213207	2.661330226	3.919370101
HIC Mean	448.6086957	438.3870968	561.125	434
HIC Std. Dev.	136.8744412	128.812183	263.0254944	138.7456548

TABLE A-5 Child Restraint Types

Child Restraint Type	Description
Infant Seat	For infants from birth to about 27 inches who weigh up to 20 pounds.
Convertible Seat	**When Used Rear Facing:**

	- All are recommended for use by infants less than 1 year and up to about 20 pounds. - Some are recommended for rear facing use, for heavier infants (30-35 pounds), and less than 1 year. **When Used Forward Facing:** - All are rated for children up to 40 pounds. - Used forward facing by children who are between 20 and 40 pounds, and over 1 year.
Combination Seat	**When Used Rear Facing:** - All are recommended for use by infants less than 1 year and up to about 20 pounds. - Some can be used for children from birth in place of a infant seat. - Some are recommended for rear facing use, for heavier infants (30-35 pounds), and less than 1 year. **When Used Forward Facing:** - All are rated for children up to 40 pounds. - Remove harness when child reaches 40 pounds and use the vehicle's adult lap and shoulder belt. - Many can be used for children up to 8 years old in place of a booster seat.
Booster Seat	- Recommended for use by children approximately 20 to 40 pounds, when used with harness. - Remove harness when child reaches 40 pounds and use the vehicle's adult lap and shoulder belt for children up to 8 years old.

www.ingramcontent.com/pod-product-compliance
Lightning Source LLC
Chambersburg PA
CBHW080921290526
45795CB00007BA/2610